William Burnes

A Manual of religious Belief

William Burnes

A Manual of religious Belief

ISBN/EAN: 9783337130114

Printed in Europe, USA, Canada, Australia, Japan

Cover: Foto ©Lupo / pixelio.de

More available books at **www.hansebooks.com**

A MANUAL

OF

RELIGIOUS BELIEF,

COMPOSED BY

WILLIAM BURNES,

(THE POET'S FATHER,)

FOR THE INSTRUCTION OF HIS CHILDREN;

WITH

BIOGRAPHICAL PREFACE.

NOW FIRST PRINTED.

KILMARNOCK:

PRINTED & PUBLISHED BY M'KIE & DRENNAN,

1875.

TO

GILBERT BURNS, ESQUIRE,

KNOCKMAROON LODGE, CHAPELIZOD,

COUNTY DUBLIN,

This Memorial

OF HIS GRANDFATHER

IS

MOST RESPECTFULLY

DEDICATED.

" From scenes like these, old SCOTIA'S grandeur springs,
    That makes her lov'd at home, rever'd abroad:
Princes and lords are but the breath of Kings,
    ' An honest man's the noblest work of GOD.' "

COTTER'S SATURDAY NIGHT.

" It's hardly in a body's pow'r,
To keep, at times, frae being sour,
To see how things are shar'd ;
How BEST O' CHIELS *are whyles in want,*
While Coofs on countless thousands rant
And ken na how to wair't."

EPISTLE TO DAVIE.

BIOGRAPHICAL
PREFACE.

DR. CURRIE, in his Life and Works of Robert Burns, published 12th April, 1800, for the benefit of the Poet's widow and children, writes, " The father of our poet is described by one who knew him towards the latter end of his life, as above the common stature, thin, and bent down with labour.   His countenance was serious and expressive, and the scanty locks on his head were grey.   He was of a religious turn of mind, and, as is usual among the Scottish peasantry, a good deal conversant in speculative theology.   *There is in Gilbert's hands, a little manual of religious belief, in the form of a dialogue between a father and his son, composed by him for the use of his children, in which the benevolence of his heart seems to have led him to soften the rigid Calvinism of the Scottish Church into something approaching to Arminianism.*   He was a devout man, and in the practise of calling his family together to

A

join in prayer. It is known that the following exquisite picture in the 'The Cotter's Saturday Night,' represents William Burnes and his family at their evening devotions.

The chearfu' Supper done, wi' ferious face,
    They, round the ingle, form a circle wide;
The Sire turns o'er, with patriarchal grace,
    The big *ha-Bible*, ance his *Father's* pride:
His bonnet rev'rently is laid afide,
    His *lyart haffets* wearin' thin and bare;
Thofe ftrains that once did sweet in ZION
            glide,
He wales a portion with judicious care;
'*And let us worſhip GOD!*' he fays with
            folemn air.

They chant their artless notes in fimple guife!
    They tune their *hearts*, by far the no-
            blest aim:
Perhaps *Dundee's* wild warbling meafure's rise,
    Or plaintive *Martyrs*, worthy of the name;
Or noble *Elgin* beets the heaven-ward flame,
    The sweeteft far of SCOTIA'S holy lays:
Compared with these, *Italian trills* are tame;
    The tickl'd ears no heart-felt raptures raise;
Nae unifon hae they, with our CREA-
            TOR'S praife.

The priest-like Father reads the sacred page,
  How *Abram* was the Friend of GOD
      on high;
Or, *Moses* bade eternal warfare wage,
  With *Amalek's* ungracious progeny;
Or how the *royal Bard* did groaning lye,
  Beneath the stroke of Heaven's avenging
      ire;
Or *Job's* pathetic plaint, and wailing cry;
  Or rapt *Isaiah's* wild, seraphic fire;
Or other *Holy Seers* that tune the *sacred lyre.*

Perhaps the *Christian Volume* is the theme,
  How *guiltless blood* for *guilty man* was shed;
How HE who bore in heaven the second
      name,
  Had not on Earth whereon to lay His head:
How His first *followers* and *servants* sped;
  The *Precepts sage* they wrote to many a
      land:
How *he*, who lone in *Patmos* banished,
  Saw in the sun a mighty angel stand;
And heard great *Bab'lon's* doom pronounc'd
      by Heaven's command.

Then kneeling down to HEAVEN'S E-
      TERNAL KING,
  The *Saint*, the *Father*, and the *Husband*
      prays:

Hope ' fprings exulting on triumphant
   wing,'
That *thus* they fhall all meet in future days :
There, ever bafk in *uncreated rays*,
 No more to figh or fhed the bitter tear,
Together hymning their CREATOR'S praife,
 In *fuch fociety*, yet ftill more dear ;
While circling Time moves round in an e-
  ternal fphere.

 * * * * * * *

Then homeward all take off their fev'ral
   way ;
The youngling *Cottagers* retire to reft :
The Parent-pair their *fecret homage* pay,
 And proffer up to Heaven the warm re-
  queft,
That HE who ftills the *raven's* clam'rous
  neft,
 And decks the *lily* fair in flow'ry pride,
Would, in the way *His Wifdom* fees the beft,
 For *them* and for their *little ones* provide ;
But chiefly, in their hearts with *Grace di-*
  vine prefide."

In Dr. Currie's Life, written by his son, we are informed that one indispensable condition of Dr. Currie undertaking to write the Life of Burns, was that Mr. John Syme of Dumfries, the faithful friend of the Poet, and Gilbert Burns, the brother of the Poet, should pay a visit to Liverpool, in order to give him such information as to the MSS., and the latter years of Burns, as it was impossible for a stranger to possess. Accordingly these two gentlemen arrived in Liverpool in the autumn of 1797. " Bound to his memory by the ties of kindred and affection, intimately acquainted with his pursuits and habits, his thoughts and feelings, they were well qualified to supply Dr. Currie with the information he desired, and which was in fact essential to the proper execution of his task. In the course of this visit of a fort-night, he accordingly obtained from them the most ample and interesting personal details, and much important assistance in the arrangement and elucidation of the numerous MSS."

Among other incidents in the family history communicated on this occasion by Gilbert Burns, was doubtless the existence of this little manual of religious belief, for without the

assurance of his own experience as a participa-
tor in the paternal instruction, it was of too
private a character to warrant Dr. Currie in
making it known, and the authority of the son
for its being composed by his father is a
sufficient guarantee for its authenticity, without
further tradition. The manuscript is in the
handwriting of John Murdoch, preceptor to
the Poet and his brother Gilbert, at Alloway.
The schoolmaster was *then* only eighteen years
of age, and his pupils comprised the children
of four neighbours, an arrangement made by
William Burnes to share the expense of inducing
Murdoch to accept the engagement, and as a
further assistance each family in turn agreed
to provide him with board. He was thus
brought into close intimacy with the Burns
family, and came to regard the father with a
filial relationship, which continued for two
years and a-half, when the school was broken
up on the family removing to the farm of
Mount Oliphant, in 1767 - the distance being
too great for regular attendance. The schoolmaster left the neighbourhood immediately
after, but returned in 1772, to teach the
English School at Ayr, when the Poet went
to board and lodge with him, to qualify himself

for instructing his brothers and sisters at home. Murdoch's attachment to the family was fostered, and his half-holidays were spent under the paternal roof of William Burnes, when he was frequently accompanied by one or two intelligent friends, that the good father might enjoy a mental feast. The recollection of those days was recalled by Murdoch in a letter, dated 22d February, 1799, printed in Dr. Currie's Life, and is a grateful tribute to the memory of good, faithful William Burnes. He writes, " The father and son sat down with us, when we enjoyed a conversation wherein solid reasoning, sensible remark, and a moderate seasoning of jocularity were so nicely blended, as to render it palatable to all parties. Mrs. Burnes, too, was of the party as much as possible, and listened to her husband with a more marked attention than to any body else.

"But still the house affairs would draw her thence
   Which ever as she could with haste dispatch,
   She'd come again, and with a greedy ear
   Devour up their discourse."

When under the necessity of being absent, she seemed to regret, as a real loss, that she had missed what the good man had said. She had the most marked esteem for her husband of any woman I ever knew. I can by no means wonder that she highly esteemed him, for I myself have always considered William Burnes as by far the best of the human race that I ever had the pleasure of becoming acquainted with, and many a worthy character I have known. He was an excellent husband, if I may judge from his assiduous attention to the ease and comfort of his worthy partner, and from her affectionate behaviour to him, as well as her unwearied attention to the duties of a mother. He was a tender and affectionate father, he took a pleasure in leading his children in the path of virtue, not in driving them, as some parents do, to the performance of duties to which they themselves are averse. He took care to find fault but very seldom, and therefore when he did rebuke, he was listened to with a kind of reverential awe, a look of disapprobation was felt, a reproof was severely so, and a stripe with the *taws*, even on the skirt of the coat, gave heart felt pain, produced a loud lamentation, and brought forth a flood of tears. He had the art of gaining the esteem and good-will of those that were labourers under him. I think I never saw him angry

but twice: the one time it was with the fore-
man of the band, for not reaping the field as
he was desired, and the other time it was with
an old man, for using smutty inuendos and
double entendre. But I must not pretend to
give you a description of all the manly qualities,
the rational and christian virtues of the venerable William Burnes. Time would fail me. I
shall only add, that he carefully practised every
known duty, and avoided everything that was
criminal; or, in the apostle's words, 'Herein did
he exercise himself in living a life void of offence
towards God and towards men.' Although I
cannot do justice to the character of this worthy
man, yet you will perceive, from these few
particulars, what kind of person had the principal part in the education of our Poet. He
spoke the English language with more propriety
(both with respect to diction and pronunciation)
than any man I ever knew, with no greater
advantages; this had a very good effect on the
boys, who began to talk and reason like men,
much sooner than their neighbours." This is
a valuable testimony to the character and intelligence of the Poet's father, written by John
Murdoch in London, twenty-seven years after
he had left Scotland, when his judgment of

men and their ways had gone through a large experience in those years. It is interesting to add, that the worthy schoolmaster lived to the venerable age of seventy-seven, having died on the 26th April, 1824. He taught English in London to several distinguished foreigners, and published a " Radical Vocabulary of the French Language," a work on the " Pronunciation and Orthography of the French Language," a " Dictionary of Distinctions," and other works, besides rendering valuable assistance to Walker in preparing his celebrated Dictionary. To the day of his death he had a tender regard for the Burns family, and was a jealous guardian of the Poet's fame and good name. His latter years were not so comfortable from reduced circumstances; but the friends and admirers of Burns made an appeal on his behalf, and money sufficient was raised to relieve his necessities. John Murdoch has a still further claim to our gratitude for having been the means of preserving this little manual of religious belief, the last legacy of his attachment to the Burns family, and not the least interesting memorial of his esteem for the worth and intelligence of good William Burnes. More than a century has passed away since the words were written down with child-like affection, and in circumstances of obscurity and extreme frugality, when the battle of life was a mere struggle for existence; and although the manuscript has ever since been treasured in the family of Gilbert Burns, and is now, with other relics, in possession of his youngest son, Gilbert Burns, Esq., of Dublin, no thought of its publication has ever been suggested to him until recently, when permission to print a limited issue has been given, to gratify some of the Poet's more enthusiastic admirers, to whom every scrap of family history is interesting. The manual is curious for its quaint phraseology, and the mould of fashion adopted at that time in similar compilations; and is still more rare, as a glimpse of that speculative theology in which the father took such delight. We are not concerned to know how far it comes up to the standard of popular belief taught a hundred years ago; or whether it is better adapted to the thought of a later period —at best, all systems of theology are but "broken lights"—and in this spirit we offer our memorial, trusting that the thoughts which William Burnes, in the devotion of his heart, compiled for his children's instruction, cannot be otherwise than acceptable as a record in the family history. Gilbert Burns' letter, written to Mrs Dunlop, at the time of the Poet's death, enters into fuller details of his father's life, he says, "My father was the son of a farmer in Kincardineshire; and had received the education common in Scotland to persons in his condition of life: he could read and write, and had some knowledge of arithmetic. His family having fallen into reduced circumstances, he was compelled to leave home in his nineteenth year, and turned his steps towards the south in quest of a livelihood. My father undertook to act as gardener, and shaped his course to Edinburgh, where he wrought hard when he could get work, passing through a variety of difficulties. He passed westward to the county of Ayr, when he engaged himself to the Laird of Fairlie, with whom he lived two years, then changed for the service of Crawford of Doonside. At length desirous of settling in life, took a perpetual lease of seven acres of land from Dr. Campbell, Ayr, with the intention of commencing nursery-man and public gardener, and built a house upon the ground with his own hands, where the Poet was born; but before making any progress, he abandoned the nursery scheme for a position as gardener and overseer to Mr. Ferguson, who purchased the estate of Doonholm. With Mr. Murdoch we learned to read English tolerably well, and to write a little. He taught us, too, the English Grammar. I was too young to profit much from his lessons in grammar; but Robert made some proficiency. My father took the farm of Mount Oliphant, and removed at Whitsuntide, 1766. It was, I think, not above two years after this, that Murdoch, our tutor and friend, left this part of the country, and there being no school near us, and our little services being useful on the farm, my father undertook to teach us arithmetic in the winter evenings, by candle-light, and in this way, my two elder sisters got all the education they received. Nothing could be more retired than our general manner of living—we rarely saw anybody but the members of our own family. There were no boys of our age, or near it, in the neighbourhood. My father was for some time almost the only companion we had. He conversed familiarly on all subjects with us as if we had been men, and was at great pains, while we accompanied him in the labours of the farm, to lead the conversation to such subjects as might tend to increase our knowledge, or confirm us in virtuous habits. He borrowed Salmon's Geographical Grammar for us, and endeavoured to make us acquainted with the situation and history of the different countries in the world; while from a book society in Ayr he procured for us the reading of 'Derham's Physico and Astro Theology,' and 'Ray's Wisdom of God in the Creation.' My father had been a subscriber to 'Stackhouse's History of the Bible,' then lately published. Our former teacher, Mr. Murdoch, came to be established teacher of English at Ayr, a circumstance of considerable importance to us — the remembrance of my father's former friendship, and his attachment to my brother, made him do everything in his power for our improvement; thus you see Mr. Murdoch was a principal means of my brother's improvement — Worthy Man!" Dr. Currie, in quoting from this letter, adds, "The reader will perceive how much the children of William Burnes were indebted to their father who was certainly a man of uncommon talents, though it does not appear that he possessed any portion of that vivid imagination for which his son was distinguished."

The Poet's remembrances of his father are full of dutiful affection. The only letter known from the son to the father, is dated Irvine, 27th Decr., 1781, and is a very remarkable one. As Jeffrey writes, " The author was then a common flax-dresser, and his father a poor peasant, yet there is not one trait of vulgarity, either in the thought or the expression, but on the contrary, a dignity and elevation of sentiment, which must have been considered as of good omen in a youth of much higher condition." After explaining the disappointment of not meeting at the New Year, he says, " I have but just time and paper to return you my grateful thanks for the lessons of virtue and piety you have given me, which were too much neglected at the time of giving them, but which, I hope, have been remembered ere it is yet too late." And three years after, writing to his cousin, James Burnes, Montrose, 17th Feby., 1784, with a notice of his father's death, he begins, " On the 13th curt., I lost the best of fathers. Though, to be sure, we have had long warning of the impending stroke, still the feelings of nature claim their part; and I cannot recollect the tender endearments, and parental lessons of the best of friends, and ablest of instructors, without feeling what perhaps the calmer dictates of reason would partly condemn." And again, in his celebrated autobiographical letter to Dr. Moore, 2nd August, 1787, the Poet gives an outline of family history. "My father was of the North of Scotland, the son of a farmer, and was thrown by early misfortunes on the world at large, where, after many years' wanderings and sojournings, he picked up a pretty large quantity of observation and experience, to which I am indebted for most of my little pretensions to wisdom. I have met with few who understood men, their manners and their ways, equal to him; but stubborn, ungainly integrity, and headlong, ungovernable irascibility, are disqualifying circumstances." It is important to notice that these remembrances of the father were written independently of each other, at different times, and without any knowledge, on the part of Murdoch or Gilbert Burns, that either had written recollections of the family history, and their first acquaintance with the Poet's letter to Dr. Moore was reading it in Dr. Currie's Life, simultaneously with their own.

" In all that has been recorded of William

Burnes," writes Robert Chambers, "we can
see the traits of one of Nature's gentlemen.
Under an exterior which extreme reserve ren-
dered somewhat repulsive, the elder Burnes
carried an intelligent mind and genial affections.
Thrown amongst people beneath him in intellect, he seems to have withdrawn into himself,
and hence it was that to an observer of a different
rank he seemed chill and austere, if not dull.
William Burnes had taken upon himself the
cares of a farm, hazarding the troubles arising
in that mode of life from want of capital, that
he might have occupation for his children at
home, instead of sending them forth to take
their chance of demoralisation amongst strangers. He exerted himself as their instructor,
and, cottager as he was, contrived to have
something like the benefits of private tuition
for his two eldest sons. The mind which
dictated such sacrifices for a high principle,
could not be one of a common mould. It is
affecting to think of the difficulties and priva-
tions which this paragon of cottage sires
encountered for the sake of his offspring, and
to reflect that by their consequences he was
made an old man before his time, and brought
down in sorrow to the grave. Of such metal,

however, were the peasantry of Scotland in those old days, which never can return." An early Biographer and personal acquaintance of the Poet—Professor Josiah Walker—in his edition of Burns, Edinburgh, 1811, bears a similar testimony to the character of William Burnes. " I have been fortunate to receive an account from one, who had both opportunity to observe, and intelligence to comprehend his peculiarities. To a stranger, at first sight, he had a chill, austere, and backward reserve, which appeared to proceed less from habitual manner, than from natural obtuseness and vacuity of intellect. But when he found a companion to his taste, with whom he could make a fair exchange of mind, he seemed to grow into a different being, or into one suddenly restored to its native element. His conversation became animated and impressive, and discovered an extent of observation, and a shrewdness and sagacity of remark, which occasioned the more gratification the less it had been expected; while the pleasing discovery made his associate eager to repair the injustice of his first impression, by imputing the repulsive manner of his reception to that series of troubles which had dulled the vivacity, and given a suspicious caution to this upright and intelligent rustic. I speak of him as he appeared at Lochlea, when misfortunes were clustering round him." The foregoing description of William Burnes was submitted to Dr. John M'Kenzie, the Poet's old Mauchline friend, then settled at Irvine, who confirms the remembrance as a correct account of the father. He writes:—" The impression which his appearance made upon me, at my first interview with him, was exactly similar to the description which he has given. When I first saw William Burns he was in very ill health, and his mind suffering from the embarrassed state of his affairs. His appearance certainly made me think him inferior, both in manner and intelligence, to the generality of those in his situation; but before leaving him, I found that I had been led to form a very false conclusion of his mental powers. After giving a short but distinct account of his indisposition, he entered upon a detail of the various causes that had gradually led to the embarrassment of his affairs; and these he detailed in such earnest language, and in so simple, candid, and pathetic a manner, as to excite both my astonishment and sympathy. His wife spoke little, but struck me as being a very sagacious woman, without any appearance of forwardness, or any of that awkwardness in her manner, which many of these people show in the presence of a stranger. Gilbert Burns partook more of the manner and appearance of the father, and Robert of the mother." Mrs. Begg's recollections of her father, as given by Robert Chambers, refer almost exclusively to his later years, when he had fallen into delicate health; but they are sufficiently distinct. " The good old man," writes the Poet's genial Biographer, " seems to have impressed his children with feelings akin to devotion towards him. It was the simple effect of his infinite tenderness towards them, and of the benevolent feeling which animated his entire conduct in life. Broken down as he was in constitution, he sustained his natural and habitual cheerfulness. He was always endeavouring to make his young ones happy by the promotion of innocent mirth, never forgetting, at the same time, any opportunity that occurred of awakening reflection, and leading them to habits of self-culture. At Lochlea, Mrs. Begg's main occupation was one suited to her tender years—that of tending the cattle in the fields. Her father would often visit her, sit down by her side, and tell her the names of the various grasses and wild flowers, as if to lose no opportunity of imparting instruction. When it thundered, she was sure he would soon come to her, because he knew that on such occasions she was apt to suffer much from terror." She remembered being at her father's bedside the morning of his death, with her brother Robert. Seeing her cry bitterly at the prospect of parting he endeavoured to speak, but could only utter a few words of comfort suitable to her years; closing with an injunction " to walk in virtue's path and shun every vice." He was troubled in spirit with a sad foreboding of the future life of Robert, and gave expression to his thoughts; but he had no presentiment of the fame which awaited his gifted son, it was simply the anxious yearning of a father's love and devotion for his children. While collating these memorials of William Burnes, we have had occasion to communicate with Mrs Begg's daughter, Isabella, in our desire to obtain a *fac-simile* of her grandfather's handwriting. In reply, she writes:—" My mother kept all she had of her father's writing with great care, she so venerated him as the best man she ever knew." The only record remaining in her possession is a book kept by him of money spent and received. His own name did not often appear in it; and the last remaining signature was sent to New York at the time of the Burns' Centenary in 1859, for the Burns' Club, after a very special request.

These simple and homely recollections sum up nearly all that has been made known of the Poet's father, who lingered out twelve years on the ungenial farm of Mount Oliphant, and removed to a more promising soil at Lochlea, in the parish of Tarbolton, at Whitsuntide, 1777, and for some years the family seemed to enjoy more comfort than at any other period of their history, all working hard on the farm. They were a remarkable family in the district, keeping more by themselves than is usual in the same class. Their superior intelligence and careful culture, with a certain refinement of manner which they maintained amid the daily toil of farm labour, caused them to be respected and looked up to as people of a superior stamp. Notwithstanding the most rigid economy, and their united efforts, the clouds of misfortune gathered round the household. The farm of Mount Oliphant had ended in difficulty, and the father was growing prematurely old with labour and anxiety, so that beginning at Lochlea was a fresh struggle to meet old demands, and, unfortunately, a dispute arose respecting the conditions of the lease, the decision of which involved his affairs in ruin. " After three years tossing and whirling in the vortex of litigation," the Poet writes, " he was just saved from the horrors of a jail by a consumption, which, after two years promise, kindly stepped in and carried him away to ' where the wicked cease from troubling and the weary are at rest.' His remains were laid in the burying-ground at Alloway Kirk, the scene of his early married life, about eight miles distant from Tarbolton. The coffin was arranged between two bearing horses, placed one after the other, and in this old fashioned mode of conveyance, usual in country districts, was followed by relations and neighbours on horseback. Alloway Kirk was a very secluded resting place in those days, " where the rude forefathers of the hamlet sleep." A few years later, and the Poet's inspiration made it famous— known all the world over—as " Alloway's Auld Haunted

Kirk," drawing visitors from all lands to share homage with "the auld clay biggin'," and the more stately Monument on the "banks and braes o' bonnie Doon," which his genius has immortalised as the Land of Burns. A simple headstone marks the grave in the rural church-yard. The original stone erected by the Poet was carried away in chips by visitors in their desire to possess some relic of the family. The present stone was renewed by Mr. David Auld, of Doonbrae, on which is inscribed the Poet's affectionate epitaph, in addition to the record of his father's death.

THIS STONE WAS ERECTED TO THE
MEMORY OF
WILLIAM BURNESS,
LATE FARMER IN LOCHLIE, PARISH OF TARBOLTON,
WHO DIED FEBY. 13, 1784, *AGED* 63 *YEARS.*
AND WAS BURIED HERE.

On the reverse side of the stone is the epitaph—

O ye whose cheek the tear of pity stains,
Draw near with pious rev'rence and attend!
Here lie the loving Husband's dear remains,
The tender Father, and the gen'rous Friend.
The pitying heart that felt for human woe;
The dauntless heart that feared no human pride;
The friend of man, to vice alone a foe;
" For ev'n his failings leaned to virtue's side."

The Family Bible Register of William Burnes.
"The big Ha'-Bible."

William Burnes was born 11th November, 1721
Agnes Broun, was born 17th March, 1732
  Married together, 15th December, 1757.

Had a son,   Robert, 25th January, 1759
Had a son,   Gilbert, 28th Septr.,   1760
Had a daughter, Agnes, 30th Septr.,   1762
Had a daughter, Anabella, 14th Novr., 1764
Had a son,   William, 30th July,   1767
Had a son,   John,   10th July,   1769
Had a daughter, Isobel, 27th June,   1771

The next entry is in the Poet's handwriting—

William Burness departed this life, 13th
February, 1784, aged 63 years, 2 months,
and 22 days.

The family name in Kincardineshire is invari-
ably spelled *Burnes*, and pronounced in the
north of Scotland in two syllables. Many
branches of the family are buried in the
churchyard of Glenbervie, all the tombstones
bearing the same name and spelling. One of
the oldest is thus inscribed :

" Here under lyes the body of James Burnes,

who was tenant in Bralinmuir, who died the 23d January, 1743, aged 87 years."

The father of William Burnes, was a farmer at Clochnahill, in the Mearns. The following extracts from the Parish Register of Dunnotter refer to his family, and shew the spelling of the name:

1725, August 18.—Robert *Burnes*, in Clochnahill, had a daughter baptized, called Elspet.

Witnesses: James *Burnes*, in Bralinmuir, in Glenbervie Parish; and James Murray, in Lumgair.

1730, August, 18.—Robert Burnes, in Clochnahill, had a daughter baptized, called Isobel.

Witnesses: George Barclay, in Nether Crigie; and George *Burnes*, in Elfhill.

1732, Oct. 26.—Robert Burnes, in Clochnahill, had a daughter baptized, called Mary.

Witnesses: George Burnes, and Mr. George Ross, in Clochnahill.

The only deviation from the family name was

by William Burness of Montrose, son of James Burnes of Hawkhill, who adopted the double *s* in deference to a relative, but afterwards returned to the original spelling. The supposition is that the Poet being the family correspondent with the Montrose relations, and noticing the double *s* used by his cousin William, may have been misled into using it as being correct. It did not alter the pronunciation of the name; but the Ayrshire people persisted in calling them *Burns*, in one syllable, as usual in the south, and so the Poet and his brother Gilbert agreed to conform to that spelling. The change was made shortly before the publication of his poems in Kilmarnock, in July, 1786—as his name is written *Robert Burness* in signing the minutes as Depute Master of the Masonic Lodge, Tarbolton, 1st March of the same year.

A MANUAL

OF

RELIGIOUS BELIEF

IN A

DIALOGUE BETWEEN FATHER & SON.

A MANUAL OF RELIGIOUS BELIEF

IN

A DIALOGUE BETWEEN FATHER AND SON.

Son. Dear Father, you have often told me, while you were initiating me into the Christian religion, that you stood bound for me, to give me a Christian education, and recommended a religious life to me. I would therefore, if you please, ask you a few questions, that may tend to confirm my faith, and clear its evidences to me.

Father. My Dear Child, with gladness I will resolve to you (so far as I am able) any question you shall ask; only with this caution, that you will believe my answers, if they are founded in the word of God.

Question. How shall I evidence to myself that there is a God?

Answer. By the works of creation: for nothing can make itself; and this fabrick of nature demonstrates its Creator to be possessed of all possible perfection, and for that cause we owe all that we have to Him.

Question. If God be possessed of all possible perfection, ought not we then to love Him, as well as fear and serve Him?

Answer. Yes; we ought to serve him out of love, for his perfections give us delightful prospects of his favour and friendship, for if we serve him out of love, we will endeavour to be like him, and God will love his own image, and if God love us, he will rejoice over us to do us good.

Question. Then one would think this were sufficient to determine all men to love God; but how shall we account for so much wickedness in the world?

Answer. God's revealed word teaches us that our first parents brake his covenant, and deprived us of the influences of his grace that were to be expected in that state, and introduced sin into the world; and the Devil, that great enemy of God and man, laying hold on this instrument, his kingdom has made great progress in the world.

Question. But has God left His own rational offspring thus, to the tyranny of His and their enemy?

Answer. No: for God hath addressed His rational creatures, by telling them in his revealed word, that the seed of the woman should bruise the head of the serpent, or Devil, or in time destroy his kingdom; and in the meantime, every one oppressed with the tyranny of the Devil, should, through the promised seed, by faith in Him, and humble supplication, and a strenuous use of their own faculties, receive such measures of Grace, in and through this method of God's conveyance, as should make them able to overcome.

Question. But by what shall I know that this is a revelation of God, and not a cunningly devised fable?

Answer. A revelation of God must have these four marks. 1, It must be worthy of God to reveal; 2, It must answer all the necessities of human nature; 3, It must be sufficiently attested by miracles; and 4, It is known by prophecies and their fulfilment. That it is worthy of God is plain, by its addressing itself to the reason of men, and plainly laying before them the dangers to which they are liable, with motives and arguments to persuade them to their duty, and promising such rewards as are fitted to promote the happiness of a rational soul. Secondly, it provides for the guilt of human nature, making an atonement by a Mediator; and for its weakness, by promising the assistance of God's spirit; and for its happiness, by promising a composure of mind, by the regulation of its faculties, and reducing the appetites and passions of the body unto the subjection of reason enlightened by the word of God, and by a resurrection of the body, and a glorification of both soul and body in heaven, and that to last through all eternity. Thirdly, as a miracle is a contradiction of the known laws of nature, demonstrating that the worker has the power of nature in his hands, and, consequently, must be God, or sent by His commission and authority from Him, to do such and such things. That this is the case in our Scriptures is evident both by the prophets, under the Old, and our Saviour under the New Testament. Whenever it served for the glory of God, or for the confirmation of their commissions, all nature was obedient to them; the elements were at their

command, also, the sun and moon, yea, life
and death.   Fourthly, that prophecies were
fulfilled at the distance of many hundreds of
years is evident by comparing the following
texts of Scripture:—Gen. xlix. 10, 11 ; Matth.
xxi. 5 ; Isa. vii. 14 ; Matth. i. 22, 23 ; Luke
i. 34 ; Isa. xl. 1 ; Matth. iii. 3 ; Mark i. 3 ;
Luke iii. 4 ; John i. 23 ; Isa. xlii. 1, 2, 3, 4.
A description of the character of Messiah in
the Old Testament Scriptures is fulfilled in all
the Evangelists.   In Isa. l. 5, His sufferings
are prophesied, and exactly fulfilled in the
New Testament, Matth. xxvi. 67, and xxvii.
26 ; and many others, as that Abraham's seed
should be strangers in a strange land four
hundred years, and being brought to Canaan,
and its accomplishment in the days of Joseph,
Moses, and Joshua.

Question.   Seeing the Scriptures are proven
to be a revelation of God to His creatures, am
not I indispensably bound to believe and obey
them ?

Answer.   Yes.

Question.   Am I equally bound to obey
all the laws delivered to Moses upon Mount
Sinai ?

Answer. No: the laws delivered to Moses are of three kinds: first, the Moral Law, which is of eternal and indispensable obligation on all ages and nations; secondly, the law of Sacrifices and Ordinances were only ordinances in which were couched types and shadows of things to come, and when that dispensation was at an end, this law ended with them, for Christ is the end of the law for righteousness; thirdly, laws that respected the Jewish commonwealth can neither be binding on us, who are not of that commonwealth, nor on the Jews, because their commonwealth is at an end.

Question. If the Moral Law be of indispensable obligation, I become bound to perfect and perpetual obedience, of which I am incapable, and on that account cannot hope to be justified and accepted with God.

Answer. The Moral Law as a rule of life, must be of indispensable obligation, but it is the glory of the Christian religion, that if we be upright in our endeavours to follow it and sincere in our repentance, upon our failing or shortcoming, we shall be accepted according to what we have, and shall increase in our strength, by the assistance of the Spirit of God co-operating with our honest endeavours.

Question. Seeing the assistance of the Spirit of God is absolutely necessary for salvation, hath not God clearly revealed by what means we may obtain this great blessing?

Answer. Yes: the Scriptures tell us that the Spirit of God is the purchase of Christ's mediatorial office; and through faith in Him, and our humble prayers to God through Christ, we shall receive such measures thereof as shall answer all our wants.

Question. What do you understand by faith?

Answer. Faith is a firm persuasion of the Divine Mission of our Lord Jesus Christ, and that He is made unto us of God, wisdom, righteousness, and complete redemption; or as He is represented to us under the notion of a root, and we the branches, deriving all from Him; or as the head, and we the members of His body; intimating to us that this is the way or channel through which God conveys His blessings to us, and we are not to expect them but in God's own way. It is therefore a matter of consequence to us, and therefore we ought with diligence to search the Scriptures, and the extent of His commission, or what they declare Him to be, and to receive him accordingly, and to acquiesce in God's plan of our salvation.

Question. By what shall I know that Jesus Christ is really the person that was prophesied of in the Old Testament; or that He was that seed of the woman that was to destroy the kingdom of Sin?

Answer. Besides the Scriptures forecited which fully prove him to be that blessed person, Christ did many miracles: he healed the sick, gave sight to the blind, made the lame to walk, raised the dead, and fed thousands with a few loaves, &c. He foretold His own death and resurrection, and the wonderful progress of his religion, in spite of all the power of the Roman Empire—and that by means of his disciples, a few poor illiterate fishermen.

Question. You speak of repentance as absolutely necessary to salvation—I would know what you mean by repentance?

Answer. I not only mean a sorrowing for sin, but a labouring to see the malignant nature of it; as setting nature at variance with herself, by placing the animal part before the rational, and thereby putting ourselves on a level with the brute beasts, the consequence of which will be an intestine war in the human frame, until the rational part be entirely weakened, which is spiritual death, which in the nature of the thing renders us unfit for the society of God's spiritual kingdom, and to see the beauty of holiness. On the contrary, setting the rational part above the animal, though it promote a war in the human frame, every conflict and victory affords us grateful reflection, and tends to compose the mind more and more, not to the utter destruction of the animal part, but to the real and true enjoyment of them, by placing Nature in the order that its Creator designed it, which in the natural consequences of the thing, promotes spiritual life, and renders us more and more fit for Christ's spiritual kingdom; and not only so, but gives animal life pleasure and joy, that we never could have had without it.

Question. I should be glad to hear you at large upon religion giving pleasure to animal life; for it is represented as taking up our cross and following Christ?

Answer. Our Lord honestly told His disciples of their danger, and what they were to expect by being His followers, that the world would hate them, and for this reason, because they were not of the world, even as He also was not of the world; but He gives them sufficient comfort, showing that He had overcome the world: as if He had said, you must arm yourselves with a resolution to fight, for if you be resolved to be my disciples, you expose the world, by setting their folly in its true light, and therefore every one who is not brought over by your example, will hate and oppose you as it hath me; but as it hath had no advantage against me, and I have overcome it, if you continue the conflict, you, by my strength, shall overcome likewise; so that this declaration of our Lord cannot damp the pleasures of life when rightly considered, but rather enlarges them. The same revelation tells us, that a religious life hath the promise of the life that now is, and that which is to come; and not only by the well regulated mind described in my last answer as tending to give pleasure and quiet, but by a firm trust in the providence of God, and by the help of an honest calling, industriously pursued, we shall receive such a portion of the comfortable things of this life as shall be fittest for promoting our eternal interest, and that under the direction of infinite wisdom and goodness; and that we shall overcome all our difficulties by being under the protection of infinite power. These considerations cannot fail to give a relish to all the pleasures of life. Besides the very nature of the thing giving pleasure to a mind so regular as I have already described, it must exalt the mind above those irregular passions that jar and are contrary one to another, and distract the mind by contrary pursuits, which is described by the Apostle with more strength in his Epistle to the Romans (Chap. 1st, from verse 26 to the end) than any words I am capable of framing; especially if we take our Lord's explanation of the parable of the tares in the field as an improvement of these doctrines, as it is in Matth. xiii., from the 37 to 44 verse; and Rev. xx., from verse 11 to the end. If these Scriptures, seriously considered, can suffer any man to be easy, judge ye, and they will remain truth, whether believed or not. Whereas, on a mind regular and having the animal part under subjection to the rational, in the very nature of the thing gives uniformity

(1)

of pursuits. The desires, rectified by the Word of God, must give clearness of judgment, soundness of mind, regular affections, whence will flow peace of conscience, good hope, through grace, that all our interests are under the care of our Heavenly Father. This gives a relish to animal life itself, this joy that no man intermeddleth with, and which is peculiar to a Christian or holy life ; and its comforts and blessings the whole Scripture is a comment upon, especially our Lord's sermon upon the Mount, Matth. v., 1-13, and its progress in the parable of the sower in the xiiith of Matthew.

www.ingramcontent.com/pod-product-compliance
Lightning Source LLC
Chambersburg PA
CBHW022037080426
42733CB00007B/871